WildWest™ Diversity

Western Legends

YESTERDAY & TODAY

African Americans 1798 to 2009

Written & Edited by:
Elizabeth Ann Lawless

PUBLISHED AND
REPRESENTATION BY:
GRAPEVINESTAR.COM

GrapevineStar™

Western Legends: Yesterday and Today...African Americans 1798-2009
Copyright © 2009 Elizabeth Ann Lawless

Tex Dunright™ brand & likeness is © & ™ Grapevine Star Entertainment Inc., All Rights Reserved
For More Info: www.TexDunright.com

No part of this publication may be reproduced or translated in an form or by any means, mechanical or electronic, including photocopying and recording or by any information storage and retrieval system, without permission in writing from author or publisher (except by a reviewer, who may quote brief passages and/or show brief video clips in review.)

Library of Congress Control Number:
ISBN: 978-0-9823177-4-7 (Paperback)

Western Legends Series: Book One

Published by:
Grapevine Star Entertainment Inc.

Co-Published by:
Wild West Diversity

Wild West Diversity is a brand of Liz Lawless Creations, Inc.

Liz Lawless Creations, Inc.
709 Mulberry
Forney, Texas 75126
www.lizlawlesscreations.com

Cover/Interior Design by: Scott Monaco / Grapevine Star Entertainment inc.
Represented by: Grapevine Star Entertainment Inc.
www.ScottMonaco.com / www.GrapevineStar.com

10 9 8 7 6 5 4 3 2 1

Dedication and Acknowledgement

We wish to dedicate this book to the countless men, women and children of all cultural groups who through their courage, determination and hope for a better life carved out a new beginning in the Western territories of what is now the United States.

These are just a few of the heroes and heroines of the past and the present times. We know that there are many more who deserve to be remembered and honored. We hope one day soon to be telling their stories.

We especially want to acknowledge our wonderful artists and photographers Lap Ngo, Fly Thomas, Doug Wiggins, Catherine Braden and Russ Aman for their contribution of capturing memories and history that might otherwise be lost.

Table of Contents

Tex Dunright™ Welcome	05
Introduction	06-07
James P. Beckwourth	08-09
Henrietta "Aunt Rittie" Foster Williams	10-11
Stagecoach Mary Fields	12-13
Bass Reeves	14-15
Cathay Williams	16-17
Bois Ikard	18-19
Emanuel Stance	20-21
Johanna July	22-23
Nat Love	24-25
Henry O. Flipper	26-29
Isaiah Mays	30-31
Benjamin Brown	32-33
Matthew "Bones" Hooks	34-35
William "Bill" Pickett	36-37
Jesse Stahl	38-39
Tex Checking In - Second Section	**40-41**
Herb Jeffries	42-45
Rufus Green, Sr.	46-47
Mrytis Dightman	48-49
Cleo Hearn	50-53
Frank White	54-55
Harold Williams	56-57
Wendell Prince	58-59
Rosieleetta "Lee" Reed	60-61
J.W. Hutson	62-63
Kenneth Pollard	64-65
Luke "Leon" Coffee	66-67
Abe Morris	68-69
Kevin Woodson	70-71
Jack Evans, Jr.	72-73
J'Lee	74-75
Doug Smiley	76-77
Conclusion	78
Autographs	79-80

Howdy! I'm Tex Dunright, The World's Favorite Cowboy™, and I'm very excited to welcome you to our community of Western Enthusiasts to discover the wonderful stories of our past & present.

These are stories rarely told outside the campfires, bunk houses or kitchen tables; however, with this book we will look at individuals who chose a different way of life during difficult times.

We hope their stories will inspire you to follow your dreams today. Be sure to visit WildWestDiversity.com to learn about future products, activities, and events!

Introduction

The adventurous saga of the American West is filled with tales of Indians, military actions, missionaries, mountain men, gamblers, pioneers, cowboys, outlaws and lawmen. In the vast lands west of the Mississippi River, they traveled the plains, conquered the mountains, built large ranches and forged towns in beautiful and desolate places.

While the government's major quest was to fulfill its Manifest Destiny, Black individuals and families saw the Old West as a place of new opportunity to enjoy a freedom that had been missing during their years on American soil.

Verbal ancestral accounts along with state and county documents and other primary resources are shedding light on the many places and faces of early black settlers. After the Civil War, many went West seeking a less hostile environment and a peaceful place to raise their families. What they found, in many cases, was a different kind of hostile environment.

It was hard, back-breaking work to farm, ranch and build communities where none had existed before. Economic, political and social challenges existed that had not been encountered before.

The dangers of terrain, rivers, forests, deserts, weather, bandits, and war parties were a different type of challenge for African American adventurers.

As the American West grew and evolved people from various walks of life continued to make their mark on the collective history of all Americans. The people in Western Legends: Yesterday and Today...African Americans 1798 to 2009 attest to the fact that courage, determination and a dream can carry you to a new place.

The heroes and heroines in these pages chose a different way of life. Those who lived in the past and those still contributing today, each have a story to tell. They lived on their own terms, creating lives out of nothing and leaving a proud legacy for future generations.

Now young and old alike can read and hear the other facts of a wild, diverse and never dull account of both African American men and women who followed their individual destinies.

James Pierson Beckwourth
1798-1866

James Pierson Beckwourth (a.k.a. Jim Beckworth, James P. Beckwith) was born in Virginia in 1798 to Sir Jennings Beckwith, a descendant of Irish and English nobility and an African American woman. His family moved to Missouri around 1809 where he attended school in St. Louis, learned blacksmithing during his teenage years, joined Gen. William Ashley's fur trapping company as a wrangler and went on his first expedition of the Rocky Mountains. Over the years Beckwourth became known as a prominent trapper and Indian fighter.

Well known for telling of his adventures, one night around the campfire a colleague Caleb Greenwood told a story of Beckwourth being the child of a Crow chief, stolen as a baby and sold to whites. This lore was widely believed and when he got caught by Crow Indians while trapping in dangerous border country he ran with it. Going so far as to marry the daughter of a chief, for the next eight or nine years he lived with the Crow and rose from a warrior to chief to leader of the Dog Clan.

He still went trapping but traded on the Arkansas River working out of Fort Vasquez and Platteville, Colorado, then established himself as an independent trader, building a trading post at Pueblo with others in Colorado. From 1844 he traded on the Old Spanish Trail between the Arkansas River and Mexican California. When the Mexican-American War began in 1846, he returned to the United States, bring 1800 stolen Mexican horses as spoils of war.

The Gold Rush saw him back in California, opening a store at Sonoma and playing cards in Sacramento. In 1850, he discovered Beckwourth Pass, the lowest mountain pass through the Sierra Nevada. In the following year he established Beckwourth Trail, a road through the mountains. The road cut out about 150 miles and dangerous passes like Donner Pass for settlers and gold seekers. The city of Marysville was suppose to fund this road but he never received payment. He could not sue for damages as a non-white. An estimated 10,000 people used the trail to enter Marysville in the following decade.

Beckwourth began ranching in the Sierra and his ranch, trading post and hotel became Beckwourth, California. In the winter of 1854/1855 Thomas D. Bonner stayed in the hotel and "The Life and Adventures of James P. Beckwourth" came out in 1856 from Harper & Brothers in New York. Beckwourth was entitled to half of the proceeds, but never got anything from Bonner. He returned to Missouri in 1859 and later settled in Denver, Colorado where he was a store keeper and local agent for Indian affairs.

The army employed him as a scout in Fort Laramie and Fort Phil Kearny in 1866. While guiding a military column in Montana, he complained of severe headaches and nosebleeds (probably hypertension). He died on October 29, 1866 at the age of 78.

> "In 1996, the city of Marysville renamed their largest park Beckwourth Riverfront Park in recognition of the debt owed by the city and Beckwourth's significance to the areas growth."

Henrietta "Aunt Rittie" Williams Foster
A Cowgirl of the Texas Costal Bend
around 1822-1926

Texas Costal Bend ranches were peopled by a unique cultural blend of Europeans, Irish, Africans, and Mexicans. One of these pioneers was Henrietta W. Foster, affectionately known as Aunt Rittie. She was born in Mississippi and brought as a slave with her sisters to the Mexico territory.

During her early life, she picked cotton, did laundry, served as a midwife, married a man named Williams and had a daughter.

Although sold as a slave to a ranch west of Victoria, she was a rare person in her time, a woman who worked cattle with men. Black women were usually confined to the fields or homesteads. She worked cattle sidesaddle and bareback on her white horse and she would go out in the cow camps with the different hands.

Gender and race (Indian & African American) made her most uncommon in the pastures of what would become Texas. Aunt Rittie had no education but she was smart and gained skill with herbal remedies as a midwife and taught others including her daughter.

Later in life she married Charles Foster and bought a place in Refugio for twenty-five dollars by paying it out a quarter a week. A person of honor and strength she was not opposed to challenging anyone.

When she thought a neighbor was trying to steal her land, she got a hammer and knocked a hole in his head. Thinking he was dead, she ran to tell the law that she had killed John Thornton, but when they went to the scene of the crime they found he wasn't dead, so she demanded they put him in jail.

Small in stature and dark in color she was known to be stubborn and ready for anything. Aunt Rittie lived into her hundreds and is buried in Refugio, Texas. It was not easy to step out of the restrictions imposed on women and blacks during that period, but she did and became a legend in the Texas Costal Bend.

Aunt Rittie, Johanna July, Cathay Williams and Mary Fields come alive at festivals, schools, museums and diversity programs through the storytelling skills of West Texas Cowgirl Rosieleetta "Lee" Reed. Reed provides living history demonstrations to children and adults.

(See her profile on page 60)

> HENRIETTA WILLIAMS FOSTER WAS A FEISTY, INDEPENDENT WOMAN WHO WAS NOT CONTENT TO DEPEND ON OTHERS, SHE PROVED HER FINANCIAL SAVVY BY PURCHASING PROPERTY AT A TIME WHEN WOMEN, ESPECIALLY BLACK WOMEN HAD FEW LEGAL RIGHTS.

"Stagecoach Mary" Fields
First African American Female to Deliver Frontier Mail
1832-1914

Born into slavery on May 15 1832 in Tennessee, Mary Fields learned how to work hard. A free spirit, she decided that slavery was not for her and ran away to Toledo, Ohio. Mother Amadeus, was the leader of the Ursuline Nuns. She was the daughter of Fields' former owner. She gave Fields work at the convent. When the nuns went west to St. Peter's Mission in Cascade, Montana; she stayed in Toledo, where she had a freedom she did not want to loose.

En route, Sister Amadeus fell seriously ill with pneumonia, Fields got word and went to Montana, to nurse her childhood friend back to good health. Sister Amadeus gave her work at the convent. She helped build the mission school and they survived many severe winters. Fields did all of the hard work. She also served as protector for the nuns.

Fields had no equal in all the west. She stood 6-foot and weighed 200-pounds. She was a cigar-smoking, gun-toting pioneer who settled her arguments with her fists, and once in a while with her six-shooter. She was never without her 38 Smith & Wesson strapped under her apron, and her shotgun was ever-ready. They said, Black Mary, as she was sometimes called, couldn't miss a thing a within 50 paces and she could whip any two men.

In the territory, she had a standing bet that she could knockout any man with one punch and she never lost that bet. Because of the extreme cold, Fields dressed like a man, except for a long dress and apron she wore over a pair of men's pants. On at least two memorable occasions, she engaged in warfare with men of the area.

Once, a neighborhood derelict made a face and other certain insulting gestures at her. Fields adorned his face with a rock, and he was last seen sprinting toward the general direction of the Canadian border. She held her own in the presence of men and beasts. One night she was returning to the mission with supplies when her horses were frightened by wolves. She was found the next morning sitting on the upturned wagon, shotgun poised, guarding her team and supplies.

On another occasion, she was involved in a shoot-out with a hired hand, as was the tradition of the Old West. Fields placed her bullet too close for his comfort, and the man took the hint and fled. After this incident, the Bishop decided her wild ways were too much and fired her. The nuns loved her in spite of her behavior. They and Mary were heartbroken at this turn of events. Although she had served the mission for 10 years, she never received a penny of compensation.

Mother Amadeus helped Fields open a restaurant in Cascade twice, and both attempts failed because she was too free-hearted with her non-paying customers. After that, Mother Amadeus asked the government to give Fields a mail route, but she had to win it first by hooking up a team of horses faster than anyone else.

She made her triumphant deliveries to the mission seated on top of the mail coach while smoking a huge cigar. She held this job for eight years, never missing a day regardless of bad terrain or freezing temperatures, and that's when she became known as "Stagecoach Mary".

When she was in her 70's she opened a laundry service, and often drank in the saloon with the men in town. Her laundry service burned down in 1912 and the residents of the town rebuilt it for her. She continued with the laundry service until her death in 1914. Stagecoach Mary Fields was buried by her friends in the cemetery at Cascade.

Bass Reeves
United States Deputy Marshal
1838-1910

Bass Reeves was born in 1838 to slave parents in Paris, Texas. After a severe physical fight over cards with his master, Reeves fled into Indian Territory where he lived with the Seminole and Creek Indians of the Five Civilized Tribes until 1863. Reeves became a crack shot with a pistol. He also became so skilled with a rifle that he was barred from competitive turkey shoots.

After the Emancipation Proclamation he was no longer a fugitive and was able to live as a free man. He bought some land in Van Buren, Arkansas, married a Texas gal Nellie Jennie, raised a family (five boys and five girls) and became a successful farmer and stockman.

In 1875, Judge Isaac C. Parker was appointed to the Federal Western District Court at Fort Smith, Arkansas. Judge Parker, better known as the Hanging Judge, selected a marshal James F. Fagan and two hundred deputies to rein in the lawlessness of the land. White outlaws had wrought the Indian territories with so much terror and violence anyone with white skin was considered an enemy.

Fagan had heard about Reeves, who knew Indian Territory so he recruited him as one of the 200 deputies commissioned by Judge Parker. Reeves was the first Black United States deputy marshal west of the Mississippi River. Due to his years living in the Indian Territory, he possessed a superior knowledge of Native languages, the people, towns and Indian Territory.

In this case, the color of his skin was a plus as it was immediately known that he was not one of the ruthless White outlaws who had plagued law abiding citizens, stagecoaches, trains and settlers. Although he arrested some of the most dangerous criminals of the time he was never shot. It was close a couple of times with both his hat and belt shot off at separate times.

Reeves made several 800-mile roundtrips from Fort Smith to Fort Reno, Fort Sill and Anadarko. When Reeves was given a stack of warrants for outlaws, he would get someone to read them to him. He could not read or write. He would memorize the warrants and then leave Fort Smith taking a wagon, cook and a posse man.

Reeves rode a large red stallion with a white blaze. he carried two Colt pistols and always wore a black hat, nice clothes and polished boots. He had the look of a lawman and was soon known throughout Indian Territory.

Reeves would often be gone for months tracking down outlaws. When he returned to Fort Smith he was paid in fees and rewards, usually $1,000 but sometimes more. After paying his expenses, he might make $400 in profit unless he collected a large reward. Reeves would then visit his family before setting out again.

Marshal Reeves had found his calling and served thirty-two years as a federal peace officer, first in Indian Territory and then pre-state Oklahoma. Marshal Reeves was known for his utmost respect and commitment to the law. He never made any exceptions to the rules, not even for his own son who became an outlaw and Reeves personally arrested for murder. During his long career he arrested over 3,000 felons and killed fourteen outlaws in gun battles.

After statehood, Reeves became a member of the Muskogee, Oklahoma police department but saw little action during his two years on the force. In 1909, he became ill and was diagnosed with Bright's disease. He died January 12, 1910 and was buried in the Union Agency Cemetery at Muskogee.

Cathay Williams / William Cathay
38th U.S. Infantry Buffalo Soldiers
{Only Documented Female}
1842-1924

A little black girl, named Cathay Williams, was born in 1842, in Independence, Missouri. Her father was a free man, but her mother was a slave; therefore, Williams spent her childhood as a house girl for a wealthy farmer.

When the Civil War broke out, Union Soldiers took Williams and several other servants to Little Rock, Arkansas. Williams worked as a cook and laundress for a Union General Sheridan until the end of the Civil War, gaining exposure to military life.

Williams needed a job after the war ended, and few opportunities were available for African-Americans, especially women. Being an independent and adventurous woman, Williams wanted to make her own money and not depend on friends or relatives. She was familiar with military life and decided to join the army so become a Buffalo Soldier.

Before 1948, it was illegal for women to serve in the military, so Williams had to pretend to be a man, and gave her name as William Cathay.

On November 15, 1866, at 22 years of age, William Cathay was officially enlisted as a Buffalo Soldier. His height was measured at 5 foot 9 inches, too tall to join the Cavalry, so she was assigned to the 38th Infantry Regiment in New Mexico.

Williams served for almost two years as a Buffalo Soldier, and during that time only her cousin and one friend knew she was a woman. In October 1868, she became ill and was sent to a military hospital. The surgeon discovered her secret, and Williams was immediately discharged from the army.

She moved to Colorado after leaving the Buffalo Soldiers and made her living by cooking and doing laundry for military families. She later moved to New Mexico where she died in 1924 at the age of 82.

Cathay Williams holds a special place in history as the only documented female Buffalo Soldier and the only documented African-American woman to serve in the U.S. Army before 1948.

(For more information about Buffalo Soldiers visit pages 26-33)

Bose Ikard
Frontiersman & Traildriver
1844-1929

Bose Ikard was born into slavery in Summerville, Mississippi in 1844. It is possible that his slave master Dr. Milton Ikard was his father and his mother was a slave named King. He lived in Union Parrish, Louisiana before moving to Texas.

The whole Ikard family, free and slave, made the moved to Texas in 1852 and settled on a cattle ranch in western Parker County on the Comanche-Kiowa frontier. It was in Texas that Ikard learned to ride and rope. As a young teenager, Ikard learn the dangers of Indian raids and the requirements of cowboy skills.

He earned his freedom by signing up for military service to the Union Army during the Civil War. After the war, in 1866, he hired out his skills and service as a traildriver to Oliver Loving. After Loving was killed fighting Comanches in New Mexico, Ikard continued four years of service with Loving's partner Charles Goodnight. They became lifelong freinds. Loving and Goodnight had been partners and pioneered the "Goodnight Loving Cattle Trail. Ikard'ss exemplary work on the Goodnight-Loving Trail and his friendships with its founders, cemented his name as a cowboy legend of the Wild West.

Goodnight said, "Bose surpassed any man I had in endurance and stamina. There was a dignity, a cleanliness and reliability about him that was wonderful. His behavior was very good in a fight. I have trusted him further than any man. He was my banker, my detective, and everything else in Colorado, New Mexico and the other wild country. When we carried money, I gave it to Bose, for a thief would never think of robbing him."

In 1869, Ikard wanted to settle in Colorado, but Goodnight persuaded him to buy a farm in Parker County, Texas, because there were so few blacks in Colorado. Ikard settled in Weatherford and began his family at a time when Indian attacks were still common in North Texas. In 1869 he participated in a running battle with Quanah Parker's Comanche band, riding alongside his former master, Milton Ikard.

Bose married a woman named Angelina in 1870, and they had fifteen children. In his later years he attended several cowboy reunions. Goodnight visited him in Weatherford whenever the opportunity arose. Ikard died at age 85 in 1929.

> THE LEGENDARY CATTLEMAN, GOODNIGHT, IMMORTALIZED IKARD WITH AN ENGRAVED MONUMENT, "BOSE IKARD SERVED WITH ME FOUR YEARS ON THE GOODNIGHT LOVING TRAIL, NEVER SHIRKED A DUTY OR DISOBEYED AN ORDER, RODE WITH ME IN MANY STAMPEDES, PARTICIPATED IN THREE ENGAGEMENTS WITH COMANCHES, SPLENDID BEHAVIOR."

Emanuel Stance
First Buffalo Soldier to Win a Medal of Honor During the Indian Wars
1847-1887

During the Civil War, 183,000 men served proudly in the United States Colored Troops with more than 33,000 paying the ultimate sacrifice. Congress commissioned some of these soldiers to Cavalry and Infantry regiments in 1866.

Emanuel Stance was born in Carroll Parish, Louisiana in 1847. He was a bright-eyed, stubborn, intelligent well-spoken man but he was little more than 5 feet tall. At age 19, Stance approached Lieutenant John Maroney, a U.S. Army recruitment officer in Lake Providence, Louisiana. Although hesitant because of his height, Stance's ability to read and write eventually persuaded the recruiter. Lt. Maroney recorded Stance's occupation as sharecropper with "black" eyes, hair and complexion.

Stance became a member of Company F, 9th U.S. Cavalry and he likely saw the U.S. Army as the quickest way to a new life. By 1867 Stance had been promoted to corporal and his company put in high gear. Literacy was a rare thing among black soldiers and his promotion likely came about because of it. Literate soldiers like Stance were made noncommissioned officers, since paperwork came with those positions.

Over the next three years, the 9th Cavalry would move around Texas to San Antonio, Fort Davis, Camp Quitman, and finally Fort McKavett. At San Antonio, the men got their first taste of frontier duty policing Indian tribes and settlers, along with protecting stage and mail routes.

At Fort Davis, Stance was promoted to sergeant and later in the year Stance's company saved a stage attacked by 100 Mescalero Indians. The Buffalo Soldiers succeeded in driving off the attackers and only lost one private and three horses.

The regiment was among those besieged by sixteen Indian attacks, all were repelled. In September of 1968, the 9th Cavalry with members of Company F successfully carried off a surprise attack against 200 Indians where only one soldier was wounded. Buffalo Soldiers killed 25 indians, wounded many more and captured 200 horses and a large amount of winter stores. If was after this that the detachment was transferred to Fort McKavett.

Although he was promoted, had responsibilities, and was the first Buffalo Soldier to win the Medal of Honor during the Indian Wars, discipline problems plagues his long military career. Stance was promoted on six occasions and demoted five times. Just six weeks after winning the Medal of Honor he was demoted in rank for fighting his first sergeant.

This literate, argumentative and determined soldier was killed in 1887 while stationed in Nebraska. It was rumored that his own men killed him after an argument, but no one was ever convicted.

Johanna July
Horse Trainer Near Eagle Pass and Rio Grande
1850-1930

Johanna July was a descendent of Black Seminoles who lived in northern Mexico near a small military colony at Nacimiento de Los Negros. The Mexican government offered land to black Seminoles to increase settlements and slow raiding comanches and bandits.

July a tall, barefoot girl wore bright homemade dresses, gold earrings and necklaces. An old pioneer, Adam Wilson, taught a young Johanna how to ride. She preferred to ride bareback with only a rope around the horses neck.

The U.S. Army, desperate for translators and scouts familiar with the border country, began to employ black Seminoles who got land in exchange for service. The July family settled near Eagle Pass where Johanna herded goats and cattle, in addition to working the horses with her father and brother.

A typical frontier town, there were no sidewalks, but Eagle Pass to

Piedras Negres (Black Rock) was a favorite Southern route during the California Gold Rush. Adventurers crossed the Rio Grande because Fort Duncan was nearby.

A military town, the War of Northern aggression was good for Eagle Pass-Piedras Negras commercial interests, where vast quantities of products shipped daily. Piedras Negras was the port of entry for all goods coming into Mexico. There was no other place in Mexico where there were so many American residents.

At 18, she married Lesley, a Seminole scout, and went to live at Fort Clark. Not use to household chores, she had a difficult time adjusting. Her husband responded with violence, so she soon left, riding her pony to Fort Duncan and returning to her mother's house.

July developed her own method of taming horses. Leading them into the Rio Grande, she grabbed their mane and eased astride. The horses nervous in the water and tired from swimming, soon lost the strength to buck and were happy to be back on dry land.

When her father died and her brother left home, she continued to work stock and tame wild horses for the U.S. Army and area ranchers.

She soon became well-known as an expert horsewoman, it was one of the few ways she could earn a living. After the death of her first husband she married two more times and continued working with horses.

Around 1910 she moved to a small house in Brackettville. She died in 1930 and is buried at the Brackettville Seminole Cemetery.

Nat Love
Deadwood Dick or Red River Dick
Champion Roper of the Western Cattle Country
1854-1921

Nat Love (Nate Love), was born a slave in Davidson County, Tennessee shortly before the Civil War. Although literacy was forbidden for slaves, Nat's father helped him learn to read and write as a child. Love's family was freed from bondage along with thousands of others after the war ended and the Emancipation Proclamation was declared by President Abraham Lincoln.

No longer confined to Tennessee, Love heard of the opportunities out West for cowhands. When he grew older he traveled there and ended up in Dodge City, Kansas where he became a cowboy. Not long after joining the Duval outfit, he began to hone his roping, herding and marksmanship skills. He later joined the Pete Gallinger company to increase his pay. Nat was an African American cowboy during the rise of the cattle business.

His story is one of adventure, courage and determination. At a time when there were few options for African Americans, he set out to explore his full potential and live his life in the American West. In 1876, he entered the Deadwood, South Dakota Rodeo on July 4th where he won the rope, throw, tie, bridle, saddle and bronco riding contests. His success at the rodeo won him the title of "Deadwood Dick" a moniker that many others carried, as it was a name from a popular adventure series of the time.

Although one third of the cowboys working the trails of the Western United States were African American, few of their names or stories were recorded. Love became the most famous "Deadwood Dick" in history and was even willing to defend the title with his life. His story of excitement and danger serves as a rare historical record of the lifestyle of an African American cowboy.

Love also impressed onlookers with his shooting skills and told how he gained not only fame but fortune to the tune of $200.00 for outshooting contestants at one competition. Hitting the bull's eye target 14 times compared to the 8 the other contestants managed. This kind of skill and money guaranteed a black cowboy equal treatment in town or on the trail.

The following year, while riding herd and rounding up stray cattle near the Gila River in Arizona, Love was captured by a band of Pima Indians. His life was spared because the Indians respected his fighting ability. After a short time in captivity, Love managed to steal a pony and escape into West Texas.

Love also had the great fortune to meet some of the most well-known legends of the West. Rough and ready individuals like Buffalo Bill, The James Brothers, Billy The Kid, Yellowstone Kelly and Kit Carson to name a few.

When he became older and the railroads began to crisscross the country, Love gave up cowboying to became a Pullman porter for a Colorado railroad company. In 1907, he wrote his autobiography, "Life and Adventures of Nat Love Better Known in the Cattle Country as 'Deadwood Dick' by Himself: a True History of Slaver Days, Life on the Great Cattle Ranges and on the Plains of the Wild and Woolly West, Based on Facts and Personal Experiences of the Author." He died in 1921 at the age of 67 in Los Angeles, California.

> QUOTE BY NAT LOVE: "I GLORIED IN THE DANGER, AND THE WILD AND FREE LIFE OF THE PLAINS, THE NEW COUNTRY I WAS CONTINUALLY TRAVERSING, AND THE MANY NEW SCENES AND INCIDENTS CONTINUALLY ARISING IN THE LIFE OF A ROUGH RIDER."

Henry O. Flipper
Second Lieutenant
First African American Graduate of West Point
1856-1940

Henry Ossian Flipper was born into slavery in 1856 at Thomasville, Georgia. His education began in the wood shop of another slave when he was eight years old. Flipper attended American Missionary Association schools during his youth and entered Atlanta University when it was established in 1869.

Flipper's dream was to become a military officer. In 1873, he wrote to newly-elected Georgia congressman James Freeman, asking to be appointed to West Point. If "qualified and worthy" Freeman would recommend Flipper.

After a series of letters were exchanged Freeman forwarded Flipper's nomination to the Secretary of War. After passing the required examinations, Flipper achieved a major step in his journey when he officially entered the academy on July 1, 1873.

The young cadet excelled at French, Spanish, law and engineering. In 1877, he was the first black to graduate from West Point. The young second lieutenant soon found himself assigned to the 10th Cavalry and stationed on the frontier at Fort Sill in Indian Territory.

While at Fort Sill, Flipper with his engineering skills was ordered to construct a new drainage system to help eliminate stagnate ponds that were blamed for increasing cases of malaria. His efforts were successful and the ditch soon bore his name. "Flipper's Ditch" was designated a National Historic Landmark in 1977.

Flipper was transferred to Fort Concho in 1880 where his troop was one of several in the field pursuing the elusive Apache chief, Victorio and his small band of warriors who were raiding on both sides of the Rio Grande.

He was then order to Fort Davis, Texas where he was assigned the duties of Acting Assistant Quartermaster and Acting Commissary of Subsistence. Things seemed to be going well for the young soldier until a particular hard commander Colonel Wiliam R. Shafer came to the post. Shafer dismissed him of his duties, then Flipper discover funds missing from his trunk. Afraid of the ill-tempered Shafer, Flipper tried to conceal the loss until the money could be found.

Flipper's efforts result in his being court-martialed, charged with embezzlement and conduct unbecoming an officer and a gentleman. His trail was held in the Fort Davis Chapel and the court found him guilty of misconduct and ordered his dismissal.

Flipper's dream of graduating from West Point was achieved but his life as a soldier cut short. However, he took his skills and become a respected surveyor. In 1890 he opened his own engineering and mining office in Arizona.

Although no longer a soldier, Flipper worked for a number of government agencies over the next 30 years, first for the Department of Justice as a special agent for the Court of Private Land Claims. He mostly translated Spanish documents into English but also appeared as an expert witness in several court cases. After a short time in Mexico and the outbreak of the Mexican Revolution he returned to El Paso.

When he returned he served as a interpreter and translator for a Senate subcommittee on foreign relations and in 1921 was appointed a special assistant to the Secretary of the Interior and worked with the Alaskan Engineering Commission. For eight years following that job he worked as a consultant for a New York based oil company.

Flipper maintained his innocence throughout his life and sought to clear his name through passage of bills by Congress. His first appeal was in 1898 and his last and eighth attempt resulted in a bill being introduced into the Senate in 1924 but it died in committee.

Throughout his life, Flipper was a prolific author, writing about scientific topics, the history of the Southwest, and his own experiences. In "The Colored Cadet at West Point" (1878) he describes his experiences at the military academy. In the posthumous "Negro Frontiersman: The Western Memoirs of Henry O. Flipper" (1964), he describes his life in Texas and Arizona after his discharge from the army.

At the age of 84, Flipper died without knowing that his rank would be restored. The Civil Rights Movement and the work of historians committed to telling all the stories of the past, brought about a review in 1976 by the U.S. Army who posthumously awarded Flipper an honorable discharge dated June 30, 1882.

> A PARDON BY PRESIDENT BILL CLINTON IN 1999 WAS THE FINAL ACT OF VINDICATION FOR THE FORMER SECOND LIEUTENANT AND FIRST BLACK GRADUATE OF WEST POINT.

Buffalo Soldier History

After the Civil War, Congress formed two black cavalry and five black infantry regiments to support the war against Indian Nations. These regiments consisted of the 9th and 10th Cavalry and the 24th, 25th, 39th 40th and 41st Infantry. Regiments included black Civil War soldiers and new recruits.

Everything from small settlements to railway construction lines were targets in need of protection. In addition to displaying their skills as military men, the soldiers helped map the American frontier, build and rebuild military outposts, and set up telegraph lines.

When the Indians encountered these black men in battle they named them Buffalo Soldiers because of their curly black hair and fierce fighting courage. These soldiers reminded them of the sacred buffalo, a worthy adversary for any warrior young or old.

Black men enlisted because it offered a consistent wage, education and opportunity to earn respect. Later on the Infantry regiments were combined to the 24th and 25th. Ten Medals of Honor were given to the Buffalo Soldiers during the Indian Wars Campaign more than any other regiment.

Although it was illegal for black women to formally join the Army, there is one documented female Buffalo Soldier but she enlisted as a man. *(See Cathay Williams story on page 16)*

Buffalo Soldiers were stationed at frontier forts and other military outposts from Texas to the Dakota territories to help with the westward expansion of the United States. These dedicated men under many harsh conditions helped build the West!

Corporal Isaiah Mays
24th U.S. Infantry Buffalo Soldiers
Medal of Honor
1858-1925

Isaiah Mays was born a slave in Virginia in 1858. He joined the Army from Columbus Barracks, Ohio and by 1889 was serving as a corporal in Company B of the 24th U.S. Infantry Regiment of the Buffalo Soldiers under the direction of Major Joseph Washington Wham.

Corporal Mays and Sergeant Benjamin Brown, also of the 24th Infantry, were awarded the Medal of Honor in 1890 for "gallantry and meritorious conduct" while defending an Army pay wagon against masked bandits near Tucson, Arizona.

In the fierce battle with the robbers, Mays, Brown and several soldiers were seriously wounded. Without the knowledge of Major Wham,

Mays, shot in both legs, walked and crawled two miles to a nearby ranch to sound the alarm.

The robbers got away with $29,000 in gold (worth nearly half a million dollars today) that was never recovered.

Mays' and Brown's gallantry caught the attention of their superiors, who said the men "behaved in the most courageous and heroic manner." The 24th U.S. Infantry Regiment was one of several famous Black "Buffalo Soldier" regiments formed after the Civil War and sent West during the Indian Wars.

Mays left the Army in 1893 and worked as a laborer in Arizona and New Mexico. In 1922, he appealed for and was denied a federal pension. Mays was eventually committed to the Arizona State Hospital, which at the time housed not only the mentally ill but also tubercular patients and indigents with nowhere else to go. Mays died at the hospital in 1925.

Mays is buried at the Hospital's "All Souls Cemetery." The oldest grave dates to Sept. 6, 1888, when Arizona was just a territory and the hospital was called the Territorial Insane Asylum.

For decades after his death, Mays' grave was marked only by a modest brick-like marker etched with a number. Mays might have been forgotten had it not been for the efforts of hospital staff and a small group of Arizona veterans who identified Mays as one of the state's recipients of the nation's highest military honor.

In 2001, Mays finally received a Medal of Honor headstone from the U.S. Department of Veterans Affairs for his bravery 110 years earlier. The headstone was unveiled just a few days before Memorial Day in 2001 at a formal ceremony with members of the American Buffalo Soldiers in attendance.

Sergeant Benjamin Brown
24th U.S. Infantry Buffalo Soldiers
Medal of Honor
1859-1910

The son of Polly and Henry Brown, Benjamin Brown was born about 1859 in Spotsylvania County, Virginia. He entered military service at Harrisburg, Pennsylvania in the 1880's and retired in 1904. He was stationed with Company C, 24th U.S. Infantry at Fort Grant and was one of only two black soldiers awarded the Medal of Honor for bravery during the frontier Indian Wars.

While serving out of Fort Grant, on May 11, 1889, along a dusty trail in Arizona, his life was changed forever. An unlikely bunch of desperadoes made off with $28,000 in gold from U.S. Army Paymaster Major Joseph Washington Wham. Buffalo Soldiers from the 24th Infantry were part of the 12-man escort that would go down fighting that day.

With a cry of "Look out you black sons of bitches!" a buckskin-clad bandit opened fire on the wagon train from an advantageous position on the bluff. The soldiers grabbed their guns and those that could took cover to return fire. Benjamin Brown and some others were struck quickly by the hail of bullets coming from the 12-15 other outlaws.

The soldiers continued to return fire, Major Wham stated that "Sergeant Brown, a naive of Spotsylvania County, made his entire fight from open ground." Brown's Medal of Honor citation reads in part that "although shot in the abdomen...did not leave the field until again wounded through both arms."

Wham, his clerk and the soldiers were ultimately forced to withdraw and the robbers succeeded in making off with the payroll in the amount of $28,345.10. Frankie Campbell, a female gambler, was ordered to stay on hand to nurse the severely wounded, including Benjamin Brown.

The money was never found, although suspects were brought to trial. While the men were charged with stealing the payroll, they were never brought to trail for the shootings, a combination of racism and local politics prevented justice being done.

Corporal Isaiah Mays, also in the battle, was the other Buffalo Soldier awarded the Medal of Honor for bravery.

Other soldiers receiving the Certificate of Merit, included Hamilton Lewis, Squire Williams, George Arrington, James Wheeler, Benjamin Burge, Thomas Hams, James Young, and Julius Harrison. These men were from the 10th Cavalry and 24th Infantry, and all were Buffalo Soldiers.

Brown never fully recovered from his wounds and carried one of the bullets inside his body until his death on December 5, 1910 at Soldier's Home in Washington, D.C.

Matthew "Bones" Hooks
First African American Member of Western Cowpunchers Association of Amarillo
1867-1951

Matthew "Bones" Hooks was born in Orangeville, Texas in 1867 to parents who were free form the bonds of slavery. As the eldest, Hooks helped his parents raise his younger siblings.

He gained the nickname "Bones" because he was so thin. At age seven he drove a butcher's meat wagon, at nine until adulthood he drove a chuck wagon and worked as a ranch hand for Steve Donald of the DSD brand.

He then joined J.R. Norris' ranch on the Pecos River, made many trail drives, raised horses with a white partner and became a top horse breaker. Cowboys kept bringing him wild horses as a challenge, until they realized there was none he couldn't ride.

He was a devoted Christian and when a ranch hand job led him to Clarendon, a primarily white community, he stayed and made it home.

While working as a cowboy, he established one of the first black churches in West Texas. He imported a preacher from Fort Worth and supposedly a congregation as well. It took years, but his amazing horsemanship skills garnered high demand and he finally won the favor of the town's residents.

He worked as a cowboy in Clarendon until 1900, when he became a porter at an Amarillo hotel. In 1910 he took a job as a porter on the Santa Fe Railroad where he worked for 20 years. He retired from the railroad in 1930 and became a civic worker in Amarillo and worked with underprivileged black youths.

His love for West Texas led him to want to bring other blacks to the area. He established North Heights, a black community northwest of Amarillo in 1930. The town boasted 35 families, a general store, an elementary school, a high school and four churches.

In his later years, Hooks participated in several pioneer, cowboy and historical gathers recounting his cowboy memories of the Old West.

His generosity toward needy friends left him penniless near the end of his life. When word came that he was ill, friends established a fund for his care. Bones Hooks died in Amarillo in 1951.

HOOKS WAS THE FIRST AFRICAN AMERICAN TO JOIN THE WESTERN COWPUNCHERS ASSOCIATION OF AMARILLO AND THE WESTERN COWBOYS ASSOCIATION OF MONTANA. HE ALSO WAS THE FIRST BLACK MAN TO SERVE ON A POTTER COUNTY GRAND JURY.

William "Bill" Pickett
Father of Bulldoggin' / Steer Wrestling
1870-1932

A legendary cowboy from Taylor, Texas, William "Bill" Pickett was of black and Indian descent. He was born December 5, 1870, to former slaves Thomas Jefferson and Mary Virginia Elizabeth Gilbert Pickett, the second of thirteen children. Pickett attended school through the fifth grade, after which he took up hard ranching work.

He participated in the Taylor fair shortly after his family moved there in 1888. Later he and his brothers started a horse-breaking business, the Pickett Brothers Bronco Busters and Rough Riders Association and offered their cowboy services.

In 1890, he married Maggie Turner, a former slave and daughter to a white southern plantation owner. They had nine children. Pickett showed his concern for the community as a member of the national guard and deacon of the Taylor Baptist Church.

Known as "The Dusky Demon" Pickett gave exhibitions in Texas and throughout the west. His performance at the Cheyenne Frontier Days (America's best-known rodeo) was spectacular. As Pickett's fame grew he was able to make a living demonstrating his bulldogging skills and other stunts. He often identified himself as Indian in order to perform, since blacks were banned from competing in rodeos.

Pickett signed on with the 101 Ranch Show in 1905 and became a full-time ranch employee in 1907, after which he moved his wife and children to Oklahoma. With his horse, Spradley, he performed across the U.S., Canada, Mexico, South America and England. He became the first black cowboy movie star when he performed in Richard E. Norman's movie "The Bull-Dogger".

One of the most memorable events in the history of rodeo involved Pickett and his hazer Will Rogers, in Madison Square Garden in New York City. The steer came racing out of the "chute" like a runaway freight-train. It headed straight for the fence, and jumped over it! Desperate to escape, people panicked. Pickett and Rogers pursued the raging steer, where Rogers was able to turn it, and Pickett grab its horns and wrestle it back down to the arena. The audience got more than their money's worth that day.

Pickett invented the cowboy sport of bulldogging after watching ranch dogs pull steers out of thorny brush. He ended his act by sinking his strong white teeth into a steer's upper lip and raising his brown hands into the air to show his only grip was teeth to lip. He would then turn the animal over by falling to one side and dragging it along with him until both came to a dusty stop.

He bought a 160-acre ranch near Ponca City, Oklahoma and died in 1932 at age 71 after being kicked in the head by a horse. Will Rogers announced his funeral on the radio.

Pickett was the first African-American to be inducted into the National Cowboy Hall of Fame. He also has been honored by the Professional Cowboys Rodeo Association and the National Cowboys of Color Museum and Hall of Fame in Fort Worth, Texas.

> Zack Miller, owner of the 101 Ranch, described Pickett as "The greatest sweat and dirt cowhand that ever lived -- bar none."

Jesse Stahl
Bronc Rider
1879-1938

Jesse Stahl was born in Tennessee in 1883. Little is known about his early years but he and his brother Ambrose began competing in Rodeos in the early 1900's.

Stahl started with steers and bulls where he won several competitions, but it was when he and another black cowboy, Ty Stokes, rode a bucking horse back to back in what was called "a suicide ride" that he found his true event.

Considered one of the greatest bronc riders ever, he never was awarded the top prizes in that event. It is widely believed that due to his color and the bias of rodeo promoters he was seldom awarded first place.

Stahl never failed to out-ride and out-show his competition. In one particular instance, he placed second in a competition that he clearly should have won outright. In a daring and deliberate move, he rode out on a wild bucking horse that had never been ridden.

The ride was magnificent and made a mockery of the judges because Stahl broke the horse called "Glass Eye" while riding it backwards!

"Although he began roping the year Stahl died, my father Rufus Green, Sr. consider Stahl one of the great black cowboys of his time. It is a shame that he was never given the recognition he deserved when he was living. Just like with my father's profile, I am pleased that people who have never heard of him will learn his history by reading these pages," said Dr. Rufus Green, Jr.

Although he retired in 1929 and settled in California, some rodeo enthusiast consider Stahl the greatest of all bronc riders.

In 1979, he was the second African American inducted into the National Western Heritage and Cowboy Museum Hall of Fame in Oklahoma City following his contemporary and rodeo pal Bill Pickett.

> Edwin Cantlon recalled seeing Stahl at the Reno Rodeo in Nevada in the 1920s: "One of the characters at the rodeo that day was a colored man named Jesse Stahl, who, because of his color, was not allowed to compete in the rodeo, but he put on an exhibition where they put the saddle on a bronc backwards, and he mounted the horse 'Tar Baby' with a suitcase in his hand. And then they turned the horse loose, and he made a real impressive ride. And his statement was, 'I'm going home.'"

Hey Partner…it's Tex again. Just checking in. We hope you enjoyed the photos and stories of individuals who lived in the 1800's when the Wild West was becoming the Western United States.

In this next section you will meet some of my good friends including: Renaissance Cowboy Herb Jeffries, Rodeo Producer Cleo Hearn, Historian Rosieletta "Lee" Reed, Pickup Man Jack Evans and Horse Trainer Doug Smiley.

Don't forget you can always catch up with me, Tex Dunright™, The World's Favorite Cowboy™ at www.TexDunright.com.

Second Section

The first section of this delightful publication was dedicated to individuals who lived in the late 1700's through the 1800's and some even into the early 1900's. These men and women, many former slaves, had traveled West where they were able to develop a sense of self, earn wages to support themselves and their families, and create new lives or homes.

A number of all-black communities grew up as individuals started buying land and settling down. These towns were in Texas, Oklahoma, Kansas, Colorado, and California. Many found work as carpenters, riders, farm hands, ranch hands, blacksmiths, ferry pilots, teamsters and cooks. When it came time for round ups and moving herds of cattle up the trail to shipping yards many African Americans participated. As mentioned previously, others enlisted in the Army and became a part of the legendary Buffalo Soldiers.

This next section of our Western Legends celebration includes individual who where born in the 1900's and many are still living today in 2009. Most of these cowboys didn't ride the range or make their mark on the land exactly, but they did make a name for themselves on the silver screen, in the rodeo, training or show arena or the spotlight of concert halls large and small.

These are a new breed of Western enthusiasts who have the same commitment to honor, accomplishment and following their dreams. They overcame obstacles of poverty, broken families, near financial ruin, but with perseverance, education and a never give up attitude, they achieved just as much as those who paved the way before them. They have proved their worthiness to be called a Western Legend.

These talented individuals enjoy telling their stories and the stories of the past so they that may continue to inspire children and adults far into the future. These Western Living Legends can often be found at rodeos, festivals, or events in the South and Western United States. Be sure and look for them. We'll see you on the trail.

Herb Jeffries
First Black Cowboy Movie Hero
Lead Singer of the Duke Ellington Band
1910-Today

Herb Jeffries entertainer, movie star, songwriter and author hardly sums up the life and times of this legend and renaissance man. Born in a Detroit ghetto to an Irish mother and a Sicilian father, Herb Jeffries is not African-American at all.

After his father died in WWI, Jeffries' mother remarried an Ethiopian jazz enthusiast. He was heavily influenced by his stepfather's passion for music, and Jeffries knew that his 4 1/2 octave range would be his ticket to success.

At 19, he auditioned for a club owner to play in an all-black jazz band. When the man questioned Jeffries' racial make-up, he spontaneously capitalized on his dark Italian features and claimed he was "Creole." He got the job, but that split decision would stay with him the rest of his life. He was discovered by Louis Armstrong and began singing with a series of Big Bands.

Touring with a Band through the South, Jeffries saw hundreds of blacks lined up at movie theaters waiting to see Gene Autry and Roy Rogers cowboy films. Recognizing a great opportunity he began thinking about how to make a Cowboy movie with black actors.

He persuaded a Hollywood producer he bumped into in a Chicago diner to make cowboy movies with black actors for black audiences. When they couldn't find a singer who could ride Jeffries ended up starring in the films (he had ridden a mule on his grandfather's farm growing up).

Jeffries starred in the movies, sang as well as performed his own stunts in a series of westerns in the late 1930's including: "Harlem on the Prairie," (1937) "Two-Gun Man from Harlem," (1938) "Harlem Rides the Range," (1939) and "The Bronze Buckaroo," (1939), where he played singing cowboy character "Bob Blake" and rode a white horse named "Star Dusk."

The films were distributed in segregated theaters throughout the South by a Dallas company. Known as the "Bronze Buckaroo," he became America's first black movie hero and provided encouragement and hope to children and adults of color during the early days of film.

In the meantime, Duke Ellington had caught "The Bronze Buckaroo" at the Apollo Theatre and in 1939 invited Jeffries to sing on stage with the band when he ran into him at a concert in Detroit.

Jeffries gave up his movie career to become the lead singer for the Duke Ellington Band and in 1942 he had a Billboard hit called "Flamingo" which went Platinum and is still selling 65 years later. Jazz lovers from all over the world also love his remarkable renditions of "Angel Eyes," "Satin Doll," and "Old Man River."

Jeffries contends that everything he knows about style and clothes he learned from Ellington, but it doesn't take long to see that he has created his own "Jeffries Style" with cowboy boots, leather vests or jackets and big cowboy hats.

His career on a role, Jeffries life was rosey but a dramatic event in 1948 almost ended it all. The plane he had borrowed from Mickey Rooney crashed on a routine flight from Las Vegas to San Fernando Valley and he seriously injured his back. Doctors wanted to operate but with no guarantees. Jeffries refused treatment.

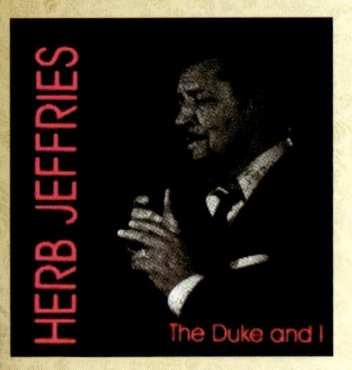

He suffered extreme pain for months until his aunt recommended a book "Autobiography of a Yogi." Being a man of action, Jeffries went to Yoganander's office and demanded an appointment. The Yogi heard the ruckus and consented to see Jeffries. He began studying yoga under the master and in eight months his pain was gone.

He still practices yoga every morning and every evening and attributes his excellent mobility to these exercises which keep him fit and ageless.

With the civil unrest in America, Jeffries traveled overseas where he found another career as a nightclub owner. Opening his own nightclub in Paris, Jeffries entertained many celebrities including Orson Welles, Ali Khan and King Farouk of Egypt.

Although he enjoyed a lucrative nightclub career, he fondly recalls his experiences as a screen and television actor. His post-War body of work in television and movies is often overlooked. Starting with the 1951 film "Disc Jockey" which boasted a host of big band personalities; he appeared in twelve pictures, four of which were made for television.

Notable television guest appearances included "Gunsmoke," "Hawaii Five-O," "I Dream of Jeannie," "The Virginian," and as the voice of the Freight Train in the 1970's cartoon series "Where's Huddles." He also composed several motion picture soundtracks. His most recent film appearance was in the 1999 American Movie Classic documentary on film preservation entitled "Keepers of the Flame."

At age eighty-one or 1995, Jeffries recorded a Nashville album of songs on the Warner Western label title "The Bronze Buckaroo Rides Again." In 2003 he was inducted into the first class of the National Cowboys of Color Museum and Hall of Fame in Fort Worth, Texas and honored at a special White House celebration during Duke Ellington month when George W. Bush was President.

In 2004, he was inducted into the Western Performers Hall of Fame at the National Cowboy & Western Heritage Museum in Oklahoma City, Oklahoma. He finally received recognition of his contribution to the motion picture industry, when he received his star on the Hollywood Walk of Fame at 6672 Hollywood Boulevard in 2005.

Jeffries continues his multifaceted career today through lectures, concerts, recordings and writings. His voice is as powerful today as it was when he broke barriers and opened up a world for many others. A vintage 99, he loves people and is still filled with unbound enthusiasm about life.

45

Rufus Green Sr.
Calf Roping Champion & Top Horse Trainer
1923-1982

Champion calf roper and top horse trainer, Rufus Green, Sr., was born in April 1923 near Edna, Texas. At the age of 15, he began his work with horses as a ranch hand with the F.W. Gross Ranch in Victoria and acquired his love for horsemanship. He learned to ride, rope, and care for horses under the tutelage of cowboy James Fry. He possessed a unique ability to communicate with horses which led him to become one of the best roping, hazing, barrel and cutting horse trainers of his time.

Weekends on the ranch were spent competing against other cowboys riding bucking horses and roping calves. Green the undisputed champion of weekend cowboy competitions, began to enter local rodeos in South Texas to supplement his income. He was so successful that he quit his ranch job and became a full-time calf roping rodeo professional in the fifties.

Green participated in rodeos all over the United States including: Arizona, Arkansas, California, Colorado, Idaho, Illinois, Indiana, Kansas, Louisiana,

Michigan, Missouri, Montana, Nebraska, Nevada, New Mexico, New York (Madison Square Garden), Oklahoma, Texas, Washington and Wyoming. He won money, saddles, trophies and belt buckles,

He was featured in Ebony Magazine in 1957 while competing at the Drumright, Oklahoma's All Black Rodeo. He was the All Around Champion at the Frank County Fair in Ottawa, Kansas in 1960 and at Manor Downs in Austin, Texas in 1978, both predominately white rodeos. At some of these events, he and his posse were the only black entrees.

During his career Green competed in over 2,000 rodeos. He was a founding member of the Southwestern Rodeo Cowboy's Association, a historically black organization. He was one of the first black cowboys to receive a Professional Rodeo Cowboy's Association (PRCA) Membership Card.

He trained over 1,000 competition and pleasure horses, as well as over 100 young men and women to compete in rodeos and horse riding competitions. Some of these young cowboys and cowgirls became top competitors such as Calvin Greeley, William Hollis, Cleo Hearn, Shirley Gladden, Paul Cleveland, Cedric Haynes and Dr. Wendell Baker. He promoted race relations and integration in Rodeo and Western Culture every where he went in America. His students, clients, and friends were multi-cultured.

As he became older he not only continued to promote rodeos, but also to compete in rodeos and calf roping events at the "senior's level." In conjunction with Monroe Lawson, Green produced the first rodeo on the campus of Prairie View A & M University in honor of black history. He touched the lives of many and left his western life-style imprint on many young people. He continued to compete and attend rodeos right up to his death. His last trophy was won at Conroe, Texas in 1978, and he died in January 1982.

He had two sons and one daughter with his first wife, Doris M. Griffin; Dr. Rufus Green Jr, Physician, Bobby L. Green, Registered Nurse, and Lawana Green-Stevenson. With his second wife, Castella Green, he had six foster children Beverly Greeley, Annette Greeley, Lawrence J. Greeley, Marcus Greeley, William Hollis and Wilton Wysinger.

Myrtis Dightman
Outstanding Bull Rider
1935-Today

Myrtis Dightman was born in Crockett, Texas in 1935 to Ada Lee and O.D. Dightman. Raised on a ranch he went to school in Crockett and learned ranching from his father. In the 1950's he moved to Houston and found a job as a truck driver. Each year he noticed rodeos came to town but there were never any black cowboys. When he questioned the organizer he was told he would be better off to start his own rodeo because the white cowboys wouldn't want blacks to compete with them.

The lack of black contestants continued to bother Dightman so against advice of friends he set his heart on competitions that would get him to the big rodeos. Although he continued to drive a truck he also started fighting bulls as a rodeo clown. In 1961 he began riding bulls and although it was difficult to get the scores to place, he earned the respect of cowboys of all races.

Dightman wasn't the first black cowboy to compete in professional rodeos but he was the first serious contender for the world title. In 1964 he placed in the top 20 and became the first black cowboy to qualify for the National Finals Rodeo (NFR). He had achieved his goal. He went to the NFR seven times and finished third in 1967, as close as he ever came to a world title.

From 1966 to 1972, Dightman missed qualifying for the NFR only once. Amazingly, Dightman didn't even pick up a bull rope until the age of 25, and he was still getting on bulls more than 2 decades later. He never won the world championship, because of the social circumstances of the time, but bull rider's will tell you he was one of the best athletes to ever sit a bull. His confidence and courage was legendary.

Dightman never had trouble with nerves before a ride. He only planned to ride until he was forty, but continued flying or driving to rodeos throughout the country for another ten years, entering as often as he could. Dightman proved he is capable of riding the "impossible" ones as well as anyone else. His career helped pave the way for other energetic black bull riders like Charles Sampson and Abe Morris.

Though the cowboys backed the talented athlete, the fans weren't always sure how to take him. When traveling, he often slept in his car rather than risk being turned away from hotels. In the dangerous world of professional rodeo, he worried more about Brahma bulls than he did about racial prejudice. This great bull rider also has one movie to his credit "J.W. Coop" starring Cliff Robertson, John Crawford and Christina Ferrare.

Dightman still runs the family ranch in Crockett, Texas. He also started a parade and rodeo in his home town in 1988 that continues today. In 1997, Dightman became the first living and third African American Cowboy to be inducted into the National Cowboy Hall of Fame in Oklahoma City. He also was inducted into the Texas Rodeo Cowboy Hall of Fame in 2001, the first class of the National Cowboys of Color Museum and Hall of Fame in Fort Worth and the Ring of Honor at the 2003 PBR Ford Built Tough World Finals in Las Vegas.

Cleo Hearn
Mr. Black Rodeo / Producer, Cowboys of Color Rodeos
First African-American to attend college on a rodeo scholarship
First African-American to win a major calf roping competition
1939-Today

Cleo Hearn was born in Seminole, Oklahoma in 1939 he planned to be a baseball star until age five when he met his first Black Cowboy, Marvel Rogers at an all Black Rodeo in Boley, Oklahoma; and a dream was born. Today he can say he lived his dream of being a professional cowboy.

A member of the Professional Rodeo Cowboy Association since 1959, he still competes today in calf roping events throughout the West and Southwest. He also produces the largest multicultural rodeo in the United States -- the Cowboys of Color Rodeo Tour which runs from April to October and visits a number of cities in the Southwest.

As a youngster he would walk a mile or two to a local barn just to be near the horses. His family still doesn't know where he got his love of horses but it might be from his father a Native American. Hearn is proud to represent two cultures and tell the stories of African Americans and Native Americans who both played a largely untold role in the settling of the American West.

When he didn't have a horse to ride, other rodeo competitors let him ride their horses. A couple of white cowboys made a huge difference in his life and career by teaching him skills and allowing him to ride their good horses when he could not afford to buy his own. Today he owns several horses and honoring those who helped him, he does the same for young cowboys coming up the trail and learning the ropes.

Due to the draft he was one of the first African American's to perform in an Army rodeo in New Jersey. He would take a bus load of soldiers with him to Cowtown Coliseum on the weekends when he served as one of the first African Americans on the Presidential Honor Guard. He also had the priviledge of standing at the Tomb of the Unknown Soldier and opening the car door for President John F. Kennedy at ceremonial occasions. He left the Army and Honor Guard to go back to college on a rodeo scholarship.

After graduating from Langston University with a degree in business and while at a rodeo in New York, he was spotted by Ford Tractors who was looking for a cowboy to appear in a commercial. He not only got the commercial, he was offered a management trainee position with Ford Motor Company where he worked for 33 years. Throughout these years he continued to rodeo on the weekends and vacations.

In 1970, he was the first African American to win the calf roping event at a major rodeo, the Denver National Western. As a cowboy he participated at all the major stock shows throughout the United States (Fort Worth, San Antonio, Houston, San Francisco, Tucson,

Phoenix, Albuquerque, and too many more to name). He even made it to Canada a time or two.

For 37 consecutive years he was a rodeo participant at the granddaddy of them all "Cheyenne Frontier Days Rodeo."

In addition to the Ford Tractor spot, he starred in commercials as a cowboy for Phillip Morris, Pepsi Cola and Levi's advertisements. Today that experience serves him well as he promotes the cowboy and rodeo lifestyle on multiple television, cable, radio, print, and Internet outlets throughout the world.

During the years, Hearn and his wife Verna, raised four boys (Harlan, Eldon, Robbie and Wendell) and they all went to college on rodeo scholarships and now work in various industries education, medical, and insurance while raising their own families. Wendell, the youngest, still competes at professional rodeos throughout the country.

For the past 30 years, Hearn and his family, wife Verna and four sons and now their families, have been working together to produce Black and Cowboys of Color Rodeos. He put on his first rodeo in 1971 in Harlem, New York for 10,000 kids. His second rodeo became an annual event and originally it was called the Texas Black Invitational Rodeo and the first beneficiary was the African American Museum in Dallas, Texas. As the tour expanded and move to other cities in the Southwest, part of the proceeds were donated to the National Cowboys of Color Museum and Hall of Fame in Fort Worth, Texas, and other local nonprofits.

Hearn was a member of the Southwest Colored Cowboys Association and helped established the American Black Cowboy Association in 1971 to encourage minorities to compete in rodeo and to become members of the PRCA.

Over the years he has been a member of the Boy Scouts of America, Lone Star High School Rodeo Association, United States Calf Roping Association, Cowboys Calf Roping Association, Old timers Rodeo Association, American Quarter Horse Association, Paint Horse Association, and the Tennessee Walking Horse Association.

Even though retired, Hearn continues to speak to K-12 students and teachers during career days, workshops and museum tours, and rodeos. He has offered the keynote address at Social Studies Conferences, Rotary Club Dinners and Sales Meetings. On a number of occasions he has participated with other educators, authors or living history experts on program panels for schools, associations, libraries and museums.

The next generation is coming along and they all have the opportunity to ride and learn rodeo skills. Hearn is hoping that one of them will pick up the reigns and continue on. Two of his grandchildren Taylor and Rachel currently compete at the Cowboys of Color Rodeos. When he is not working with them he is mentoring other junior calf ropers and barrel racers.

Throughout his rodeo career, Hearn has often been interviewed some of the highlights include: 2003 Forgotten Cowboys — British Broadcasting Corporation Documentary Cowboys of Color Rodeo at the State Fair of Texas; 2004 Cowboys of Color Rodeo Tour Best of the Best — TV1 Cable Broadcast; Dan Rather CBS Nightly News; and numerous appearances on ABC, NBC, CBS, and FOX.

Hearn has been recognized for his outstanding achievements as the: 2005 Texas Trail of Fame Inductee - Fort Worth Stockyards; 2006 Nominee for Texas Black Sports Hall of Fame, African American Museum Dallas; and in 2009 as an inductee into the first Bandera Museum Hall of Fame.

> "CLEO HEARN IS MY HERO. AFTER WE MET HIM, MY WIFE AND I COMPLETELY IMMERSED OURSELVES IN THE WESTERN LIFESTYLE. THE THINGS HE HAS ACCOMPLISHED MAKE US PROUD." COMMENTED PASTOR RANDOLPH SUDLER.

Frank White
Tennessee Walking Horse Champion
1940-Today

Born into a poor Jackson, Mississippi, neighborhood in 1940, Frank White was one of nine children supported by his mother's $3 per week salary. White abandoned school and taunting schoolmates in grade school choosing to care for his brothers and sisters. When he was 12 he snuck a ride on a Tennessee Walking Horse and when the owner caught him instead of being punished he was offered a job for $5 per week.

An old man there counseled the youngster to learn all he could about horses and never to settle for being second-best. White lived in constant fear that someone would discover his secret. He concentrated on the horses, because they didn't care if he could read or write or worry about his hand-me-down clothes. His soft touch and gentle voice soon made him many friends in the stables.

For more than fifty years, with a healthy measure of humility and southern charm, White squeaked by on the Christian principles and self-worth taught by his mother. His knack for training Tennessee Walking Horses and gaining the attention and affection of wealthy people who owned them brought him equestrian success.

Although he never finished school, those qualities taught by his mother served White well, enabling him to become one of the most highly acclaimed Walking Horse Trainers in the country and owner of Frank White Stables and Training Center south of Junction City, Oregon.

His place in Walking Horse history was clinched in 1993 when he and a flashy bronze-colored mare named "In The Limelight" finished at the top in both harness and plantation riding classes at the Tennessee Walking Horse Celebration in Shelbyville, Tennessee. The "World Championship" of the sport which attracts over 3,000 horses annually and tens of thousands of spectators.

White was the first black trainer so honored in a field dominated for decades by wealthy whites. The walls of his office are lined with trophies, ribbons and awards – evidence of the hard work and dedication he's put into achieving goals and dreams formed during his early childhood years in Mississippi.

Today he host clinics around the country to shoe, train, and ride Tennessee Walking Horses, as well as does exhibitions for public schools to teach the children about the horse, motivate them to stay in school, get a good education, while seeking to achieve their goals. He is in demand as a motivational speaker and shares the lessons he's learned with students at all levels.

As a Spokesman for Adult Literacy, White is learning to read and write and doing quite well. Just like he never gave up on his dreams of winning top riding honors at Shelbyvillle, he has no intentions of giving up literacy now that he is on the education trail!

55

Harold Williams
Wrangler Pro-Rodeo Judge, Paralegal and Horse Trainer
1940-Today

Harold Williams grew up in Dallas went to high school then joined the Marine Corps where he was sent to Vietnam. After serving two years he came back to the States to go to college at Pepperdine University in Los Angeles, California and University of Dallas where he became a paralegal.

He actually started his legal work while in the Marine Corps and just continued in the civilian world where he worked for corporate lawyers on Federal Court cases. Dealing with judges was a lot like working with Generals. Although he didn't like the rush rush aspect nor being indoors so much, he had a family and kids to consider. They actually closed three of the firms he was with but he worked with one of the partners who always asked him to go with him to the next location.

His grandparents and uncles had a farm over in Commerce, Texas so he grew up around horses and cows. "They weren't much for gambling with the grocery money, which is what they thought of rodeo and entry fees," said Williams. So he didn't start his rodeo career until he was in the Marine Corps where they had rodeos between the different service branches.

Many of the bases built their own rodeo arenas like Camp Pendleton. There was always something going on in the arena. Williams being a curious sort went to see what was happening and was captured. He knew stock but not much about rodeo. He started as a bulldogger or steer wrestler and team roper which was big in California.

When injuries kept him from competing he would come and work for Cleo Hearn's Cowboys of Color Rodeos handling the stock. Watching the judges, sparked his interest and it just evolved into another way to stay in the sport he loved. "All it took was a want and some reading, which as a paralegal I had done plenty of reading," said Williams.

As a Wrangler Pro-Rodeo Judge he had to become certified and is one of only two African American Pro-Rodeo Judges in the country. He travels all around the country now and mentors up and coming young black men who want to go the Judging route. Mostly it is about being prepared. Williams is working with a young man from Arkansas right now.

After his daughter graduated from college, he was able to retire from the legal profession, and go back to pursuing his passion for horses as a Wrangler at the DD Ranch in Mesquite, Texas. Between caring for 10-20 horses at any given time and traveling the rodeo circuit, Williams manages to keep busy.

Wendell Prince, Sr.
Texas Buffalo Soldier Living History Programs
1942-Today

Wendell Prince, Sr. was born into a farming family in Hammond, Texas in 1942. Shortly after that his family moved to Dallas were he was raised, married his high school sweetheart Minnie, had five children and worked at Bishop College.

In 1966 he moved to Inglewood, California with his company GSI (a Texas Instruments subsidiary) handling records for oil and water explorations. He then went to work for McDonald Douglas as a machinist and supervisor where he remained for many years.

When his mother became ill, he moved back to Texas and operated M&S Roofing for 20 years before retiring. While working in the roofing business he joined the Bear Creek Buffalo Soldiers Youth

Organization in Irving, Texas. That began a wonderful relationship providing living history demonstrations under the encouragement and direction of Cap. Kenneth Pollard, Texas Parks & Wildlife Education and Outreach Division.

Now that he is retired he serves as Vice President and Historian for Bear Creek. He travels through the State of Texas giving Buffalo Soldier presentations at schools, museums, libraries, camps, churches, corporations and other organizations.

In addition, he represents the Infantry while others portray the Calvary at Cowboys of Color Rodeos and for ICREA, Inc. a 501(c)(3) education nonprofit who provides programs for juvenile justice centers, recreation centers, teen summits and other facilities and events.

Prince is happy to tell the stories to anyone who wants to know about the three decades of history that many people have forgotten (1866 to 1896). Stories about the men of the 24th infantry, men like Benjamin Brown and Isaiah Mays, who fought as Buffalo Soldiers in the Western and Indian territories after the Civil War.

He has received numerous awards and certificates for his Buffalo Soldier presentations that cover what an Officer's tent looked like; what the troopers had to carry in the field including food, weapons, clothing and blankets; where and how they escorted officers, their families and other pioneers, how they kept them safe on the frontier and what they received as pay.

> "THERE IS SO MUCH FORGOTTEN HISTORY TO BE LEARNED FOR BOTH THE YOUNG AND THE OLD. I AM HONORED TO BE ABLE TO SHARE EVEN A SMALL PART WITH CURIOUS INDIVIDUALS OR GROUPS. UNTIL WE MEET, HAPPY TRAILS TO YOU," WENDELL PRINCE, SR.

Rosieleetta "Lee" Reed
West Texas Cowgirl
Living History Storyteller
1950-Today

Rosieleetta "Lee" Reed was born to Lugene and Julia Johnson Reed while her father was stationed with the Army in Japan. They moved to Amarillo, Texas when she was a child. Most people thought she was a boy because she was always out riding horses, herding cattle or going to town with her father. She wore her jeans, boots and cowboy hat proudly from the time she was a small child.

After high school, Reed attended Amarillo Junior College and received her Nursing Certificate. She moved to Dallas to work at Methodist Hospital because they had the most progressive heart and lung trauma program in the State. She worked a short stint at Presbyterian before finding her home at Medical City Hospital Dallas.

Throughout her life she has continued to ride horses and spend her free time living and teaching both youth and adults about the Western lifestyle. She is the founder and CEO of Lakeside Riders in Fort Worth, Texas, a non-profit organization that promotes youth academics, responsibility, and community service through equestrian after school, weekends and scholarship programs. The club is located in the Stop Six African American community in Southeast Fort Worth.

Reed was the 2005 NBC 5 - Jefferson Awards Regional Grand Prize Winner and she received the 2005 National Jacqueline Onassis Award for Public Service by an Individual out of numerous entries throughout the United States, after being nominated by the Dallas NBC 5 station. She was the winner of the First Humanitarian Award at Medical City Hospital Dallas, Texas where she has been employed for more than 30 years.

During 2006 she was inducted into the National Cowboys of Color Hall of Fame and received the 2006 A. Maceo Smith Community Service Award for Youth Involvement. She was the health coordinator for the Historic Huff Wagon Train Project and provides living history demonstrations and programs about the roles of Frontier Women for Education and Outreach Program of the Texas State Parks Division, Texas Park & Wildlife Department.

Reed has conducted living history programs around Texas at the Panhandle Plains Museum in Canyon, the National Cowboys of Color Museum and Hall of Fame in Fort Worth, the African American Museum in Dallas, the Cowboy Artist of America Museum in Kerrville, and the George Bush Memorial Library in College Station.

She travels statewide as a trooper in the Texas Buffalo Soldier Regiment conducting programs in Texas schools and other public venues. She has been recognized as a Docent for Fort McKavett, the Cowboys of Color Rodeo Tour, and the George Bush Memorial Library for research and presentations about the role of black cowboys and cowgirls.

Reed specializes in presentations about Williams Cathy, also known as Cathay Williams, "Stagecoach Mary" Fields, Henrietta "Aunt Rittie" Foster Williams and Johanna July, black females who where born during the mid to late 1800's.

J. W. Hutson
Rodeo Cowboy, Rodeo Judge, Teacher & Actor
1950-Today

J.W. Hutson was born and raised in one of the oldest black neighborhoods in Fort Worth, Texas. His father worked for Joe Johnson a rancher in Kennedale, Texas so from age four he always had a horse of his own to ride.

When he was fifteen, he met some cowboys at the Circle L5 Rodeo and spent the day with them. He was so impressed that he developed an interest in bulldoggin' the rodeo event made famous by black Texas cowboy Bill Pickett. However, he didn't have a rodeo horse, just a pleasure mount, nor did he have a place or anyone to teach him the specifics.

When they suggested he get a riggin' and become a bareback rider, that is what he did. Hutson rode bareback horses at rodeos for eight years throughout high school, college and even after he started working professionally.

After high school, Hutson had attended North Texas University were he obtained his teaching degree in English, Speech and Drama. He started his teaching career with Fort Worth Independent School District where he worked for twenty two years before going to work for Dallas Independent School District for eight years. Throughout those years he continued to rodeo on the weekends and summers.

He added calf roping to his repertoire when he ran into Hardy Tadlock and John South in Denton and they invited him to come rope. Over the years he has won the tie-down roping at the 1992 Texas Black Invitational Rodeo in Dallas where rodeo proceeds benefit the African American Museum in Fair Park. He also won the Rolan Reid D Roping in 1995 and won Incentive Division of the Original Calf Roping Association in 1999.

When the Texas Black Rodeo Tour transitioned into the Cowboys of Color Rodeo Tour to be more inclusive of other minorities and anglo competitors, Hutson became a judge for the organization and worked at rodeos throughout the Southwest including: Fort Worth, Houston, San Antonio, Paris, Austin, Oklahoma City and the National Finals at Mesquite.

During a rodeo in Oklahoma, Calf Roper Cleo Hearn, told him about working in commercials and being the Marlboro Man, and what a kick it was to see his face on a 30 foot billboard. The next Monday Hutson called a local talent agent and begin doing commercial work.

His acting appearances include: Unsolved Mysteries, 2002 Cowboys of Color Calendar and commercials for Texaco, Conoco, Texas Lotto, and Texas Tourism. Recently retired from teaching, he still attends rodeos, judges rodeos and is available for commercial projects.

Captain Kenneth Pollard
Chaplain Texas Buffalo Soldiers
Texas Parks & Wildlife Education & Outreach
1952-Today

Kenneth Pollard was born in Meridian, Texas in 1952. As a young boy he grew up watching too much Sea Hunt, Rin Tin Tin and Wild Kingdom. When he got older he realized he could do all of that and get paid for it. Working for the Texas Parks and Wildlife department, Pollard has lived his dream. "I love to get up and come to work every day," he said.

After twenty years and various positions with Texas Parks and Wildlife, in 1994, Pollard realized a way to reach minority youth and families across Texas. The plan included a volunteer group in Abilene Texas, the "Soldiers in Blue Committee" who assisted Pollard in the development of a statewide educational program for the Texas Parks and Wildlife Department that emphasizes a shared Texas Heritage.

Captain Pollard is the Commanding Officer and Chaplain for the Texas Buffalo Soldiers Regiment and works with groups throughout Texas to educate children and adults. The Regiment is composed of a statewide network of Buffalo Soldiers, Black Cowboys, Mexican Cowboys, European

Cowboys, American Indians, Frontier Women and other cultural groups from across Texas.

Members of the Regiment demonstrate the shared heritage of Texas through living history programs, wagon train & trail rides, youth and family camp outs, rodeos and other venues. Youth and families have the opportunity to participate through hands-on outdoors educational and recreational activities.

The Texas Buffalo Soldiers Regiment has conducted programs to more than 3,000,000 youth and families across Texas over the past 15 years. Pollard has been involved in videos, movies and documentaries including the Discovery Channel, TNT-The Rough Riders, Texas Education Agency Network, Fox Sports Southwest and numerous television and radio shows.

The Texas Buffalo Soldiers Heritage Trail Project is an umbrella program designed to bring education, preservation, tourism and other social-economic opportunities to minority communities and citizens.

During the 76th Legislative Session Dr. A.C. Jackson of Abilene, Pollard and other members of the Texas Buffalo Soldiers were honored on the floor of the Senate by the Honorable Senator Royce West and the House of Representatives by the Honorable State Representative Dr. Bob Hunter. They were recognized for the development of the Texas Buffalo Soldiers Program and their testimony and support assisted the members of the 76th Legislative session with the passage of Senate Bill 1457, designating the month of July "Texas' Buffalo Soldiers Heritage Month".

From 2000 to 2009 Pollard has overseen the Buffalo Soldier participation at Cowboys of Color Rodeos held every year from April through October. Texas Buffalo Soldier groups from around the state have participated at rodeos in Dallas, Austin, San Antonio, Houston, Fort Worth and Mesquite teaching children and adults about the days of the late 1800's when adventurers built new lives in the Western territory.

In 2006, Pollard was inducted into the National Cowboys of Color Museum and Hall of Fame for his contributions to multicultural history and providing living history demonstrations, artifacts, uniforms, journals, animals, equipment and personnel for educating people of all ages about our collective Western heritage.

In 2008 the Texas Buffalo Soldier program was transferred to the Texas Historical Commission, where the Regiment continues to operate in the interest of the citizens and visitors who come to enjoy the history, culture and outdoor resources of this great State.

Luke "Leon" Coffee
World Famous Rodeo Clown and Army Veteran
1954-Today

Luke "Leon" Coffee was born in Blanco, Texas in 1954. Coffee comes from a line of farrier and horse-training folk, and when he was not in the arena, he was shoeing and training horses. A world-famous Rodeo Clown, Coffee has a list of accomplishments. A United States Army veteran, bullfighter, and "man in the can," the lifetime gold card member of the Professional Rodeo Cowboys Association (PRCA) since 1973, he has TV, rodeo commentary, documentaries, commercials, and even movies (including "8 Seconds," "My Heroes Have Always Been Cowboys," and "Jericho 2001") to his credit.

He has been featured on the covers of many leading newspapers and magazines. He has worked the National Finals Rodeo in four different decades, two different centuries, and two different millenniums with his familiar green hat and happy face. His mule act Hippie Motorcycle has also captured the attention of thousands of fans in the stands.

Coffee has delighted crowds and helped protect contesting cowboys for over 30 years. He was repeatedly selected as a barrel man and bullfighter for the PRCA and the National Finals Rodeo (NFR) in Las Vegas, Nevada. Coffee was named PRCA Clown of the Year in 1983 and has continued to be honored for his humor by being one of the top three candidates for Clown of the Year from 1984-2001.

In February 2004, Coffee was inducted into the Texas Rodeo Cowboy Hall of Fame in Belton, Texas, for his more than thirty (30) years of service to the rodeo industry. Coffee has participated in major annual rodeos throughout Texas. He was selected as the barrel man for the inaugural Pace Championship event in Las Vegas, in 2000.

Coffee celebrated his 25th year of participating in Nampa, Idaho's 90th Annual Snake River Stamped in July 2005. He also performed at multiple Cheyenne Frontier Days, and was the Lone Star Circuit Finals Rodeo bullfighter 1980, '82; USSTC Cup Finale (Dallas) barrel man 2001-02; Pace Classic (Dallas) barrel man 2003; USSTC Cup Finale (Las Vegas) barrel man 2000; Wrangler Bullfight Tour Finals barrel man 1999; and Texas Circuit Finals Rodeo 1980-82, '92, '96, '97.

In addition, Coffee is known for his charity work almost as much as for his antics at the rodeo. He has participated in charity rodeos throughout his career and could always be found visiting the children's wards of local hospitals during his rodeo travels. He retired from bullfighting in 2008. "I don't know how to be a spectator, but I guess I'm going to have to learn," the longtime rodeo clown said. "My knees are so bad, I just don't have the ability to entertain the people in the stands like I use to".

> WHEN ASKED ABOUT HIS CAREER, THIS AUSTIN, TEXAS, WORLD FAMOUS RODEO CLOWN, BULLFIGHTER AND BARREL MAN SAYS "I WOULDN'T TRADE WHAT I'VE DONE FOR A MILLION DOLLARS. I'VE DELIVERED A LOT OF JOY. I'VE DELIVERED A LOT OF SMILES," HE SAID.

Abe Morris
Bull Rider, PRCA Rodeo Announcer, Columnist & Author
1956-Today

Abe Morris was raised in Woodstown, New Jersey. In 1964, at the age of eight he began riding roping calves at the Cowtown Rodeo then progressed to riding junior bulls.

After graduating from Woodstown High School in 1974, he ventured West to attend the University of Wyoming on athletic and rodeo scholarships. Morris competed for four years for the University of Wyoming as a bull rider on the university's championship rodeo team and was a member of the National Intercollegiate Rodeo Association.

A highlight of Morris' career was winning the bull riding title in the 1978 Laramie River Rendezvous Rodeo held at the University of Wyoming Field house.

Morris competed for several years in the Mountain States Circuit Finals Rodeo and the Dodge National Circuit Finals Rodeo as a member of the Professional Rodeo Cowboy Association (PRCA).

Morris can stake his claim in rodeo history as a former champion bull rider. Morris is a 1980 graduate of the University of Wyoming (UW) with a bachelor's degree in business management.

He spent nearly 25 years riding bulls on the college and professional rodeo circuit until an injury in August 1994 ended his career.

However, Morris kept his hat in the arena writing a monthly column for "Humps N' Horns Bull Riding News," and getting his certification to announce PRCA approved rodeos. He is the first African American to hold an announcer's card with the PRCA.

He spent nine years as a broadcast commentator for the world famous Cheyenne (Wyoming) Frontier Days for Prime Sports and FOX Sports Network.

In 2005 he published his first book, "My Cowboy Hat Still Fits: My Life as a Rodeo Star," which chronicles his days as a black professional rodeo cowboy.

Today Morris spends his days working as a licensed and registered representative in financial services along with making book appearances detailing the stories of his rodeo days. He also speaks to youth and adults offering his story as motivation for pursuing and achieving dreams.

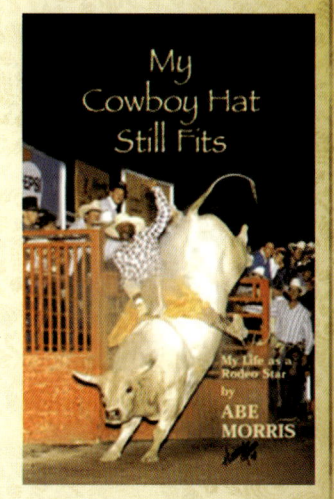

Morris continues to write articles and is on his fourth book. He lives in Denver, Colorado with his son Justin.

Kevin Woodson
Cowboys of Color Rodeo Announcer
and Former Bullfighter
1956-Today

Kevin Woodson was born in St. Louis, Missouri in 1956, and always had a passion for horses. He attended his first rodeo at age 2, and fell in love with rodeo, especially the "rodeo clowns". After excelling in baseball, football and hockey, he attained his goal of becoming a rodeo bullfighter.

He began his rodeo career after attending a bullfighting school at the Archview Stables Arena in Belleville, Illinois where the "best student" of the school helped the seasoned bullfighters at the weekly Saturday night bull buck out.

He teamed up with fellow bullfighter Maurice File, and the two were the featured "life savers" for the Saturday night bull riding being paid a paltry 50 cents per bull. The pay got better as he earned his way to open and pro sanctioned rodeos in Missouri, Illinois, Tennessee and Georgia.

Woodson was selected as the bullfighter for the Illinois High School Regional, Multi-State Regional and Finals Rodeos nine years in a row, a work relocation interrupted his 10th year. He was selected as one of the bullfighters for the Bill Pickett Invitational Finals Rodeo 2 years straight (1992 and 1993). His move to Texas with family resulted in retirement from fighting bulls.

Today he competes in calf roping and is the voice of the Cowboys of Color Rodeo Tour that highlights the contributions of minorities to the Western expansion. Rodeo is a family affair at the Woodson ranch, since daughter Leah competed as a barrel racer from age 8 until she started college.

The Cowboys of Color Rodeo gives ethnic cowboys and cowgirls an opportunity to excel at their chosen sport, earn prize money and be positive role models to future generations. The audience is treated to a double bonus -- fast paced thrills and spills while getting an education about the untold contributions that Blacks, Hispanics and Indians made to the settling of the West.

Professionally, Woodson works as a radio broadcaster for Citadel Broadcasting, formerly the ABC Satellite Network, and has worked in the industry for 26 years. He has worked with the Tom Joyner Morning Show, Doug Banks Morning Show, Ricky Smiley Morning Show, "The Touch," and as host of stations and shows numbering too many to mention. "Rodeo fans are the most loyal fans of any group I know except for Rodeo fans."

Woodson also speaks to youth about their heritage, the importance of finding something they love and committing their energies to being the best that they can be at that activity, whether it is a sport, a job or a community endeavor.

Jack Evans, Jr.
Author, Rodeo Stock Contractor and Cowboys of Color Rodeo Pick-up Man
1960-Today

Jack Evans, Jr. was born in Portales, New Mexico in 1960 to Patricia and Jack Evans, Sr. His father is currently the President of Southwestern Christian College in Terrell, Texas, a coeducational liberal arts college which also offers a bachelor's degree in biblical studies.

He graduated from Terrell High School, Southwestern Christian College and Abilene Christian University before taking up his current position as assistant to the President of Development at Southwestern Christian College.

In addition to his work at the College, Evans is an internationally known public and motivational speaker; an ambassador for Christ at Lake Como Church of Christ; and an ambassador for rodeo as a stock contractor and pick up man.

Evans briefly rode bareback horses but found he liked working on the other side of the rodeo action as part of the team that makes the rodeo happen.

As the pick up man for the Cowboys of Color Rodeo Tour he helps bareback riders dismount safely and rounds up stock after a ride. He provided similar services for the Women's National Finals Rodeo held in Fort Worth.

"Most people don't realize that more guys get hurt riding bareback horses than bulls. It can really jerk you around if you don't have good technique. And getting off…oh boy…you want a guy like Jack Evans helping you dismount safely," Rodeo Producer Cleo Hearn said.

As a rodeo producer and stock contractor, Evans maintains a ranch just east of Dallas. He has had several bucking horses receive "Bucking Horse of the Year" on the High School Rodeo Circuit.

Evans is the author of eight books for the spiritual market, the most recent one "The God of a Second Chance," he travels widely promoting his books and positive lifestyle messages.

"People are often surprised when they find out about my Western lifestyle," Evans said. "I also like hunting and fishing, it feeds my spirit, it's not just my passion but my obsession."

J'Lee
Country Rodeo Singer & Songwriter
1961-Today

J'Lee was born and raised in East Palatka, Florida, the youngest of thirteen. J'Lee's mother (Aretha Peoples) passed away when she was eleven. Years later her father (Jaufees Peoples) married Lula Mae who J'Lee calls the "greatest stepmother on earth." Her stepmother remains a loving and supportive person in her life.

J'Lee grew up in the country with the hogs, chickens and ducks. But horses always had a special place in her heart. The highlight of J'Lee's childhood was coming home from elementary school and her daddy had bought her a horse. "I remember it like it was yesterday. That was the most exciting moment in my life." J'Lee still believes "Horses are the most beautiful animals on earth."

J'Lee also had a second love – music. All kinds of music: pop, rock, gospel, r&b, country and more. She grew up singing in church. While growing up, J'Lee would rejoice when others got a call, however, she always asked, "but God, what am I suppose to do?" It was vital to her to know what she could do to touch people in a positive way, to share God's grace.

She began to dream of songs she'd never heard before but couldn't remember when waking. After a year something special happened, she began to hear and remember the lyrics and melody after waking. This was God's message to her. Her passion is writing songs and singing to make people smile or touch their lives with her music.

In 1995, she moved to Nashville, Tennessee, to learn more about the business side of the music industry. J'Lee has a sound of her own; her music is a mixture of country energized with a pop-rocking flavor enriched with soulfulness. Her style emerged from listening to diverse genres of music. Now when she creates music all those sounds collide into what you might call "J'Lee's Style."

She came to love rodeo and equestrian events by watching the horses and bulls perform. These animals were true athletes. Her first Music Row charted song "Cutting Horse Dance" was written after being mesmerized by watching a horse and rider compete. It's a catchy, feel good, make you wanna dance song.

Her CD "Offbeat Rodeo" is helping to pioneer the role of black women in country and cowboy music. One well-received song "The Roughest Ride" surprises people when they realize it is the bull talking. As a child she dreamed about a bull that was always close but never tried to harm her. Which might account for her empathy with rodeo bulls. Also her father was a big Western movie fan.

J'Lee really enjoys watching people respond to her music. When they sing along with the words and dance to her music, it makes her smile!

She has been profiled in a number of national Western magazines and performs at well-known equestrian and rodeo events throughout the South and Southwest. Look for J'Lee at a rodeo near you.

Doug Smiley, Jr.
Owner Five Star Farms
Tennessee Walking Horse Trainer & Competitor
1975-Today

Doug Smiley, Jr. was born in Flint, Michigan in 1975. Growing up there was always a horse around. His earliest connection was a painting of a palomino and white his father had hanging in the basement. "I looked at the horse and I could see its soul."

Smiley wasn't born on a Tennessee Walking Horse but he arrived their quickly. Smiley came by his love of Walkers honestly. His father, Doug Smiley Sr. has bred, trained, and shown the versatile breed for many years. From the age of 4-12 any chance Smiley had to ride he took it. Hours seemed like minutes and he could have slept on the horse if his father would have let him.

In high school and college, horses took a backseat and traditional sports become Smileys' focus (football, basketball, and soccer). When his father had a stroke which paralyzed his left side, Smiley often checked on the horses, until he recovered. Instantly his passion for horses was ignited again.

His father was one of the reasons that he rode and he always told his son to be his own man. As good a horseman as his father was and as much as he taught him about horses, the most valuable lesson was not what he could do from the saddle but what kind of man would he be on the ground.

Before returning to the equestrian business, Smiley worked as a child psychologist for the Boys and Girls Club of North Texas. When he returned to the horse business, he joined Walkers West, in Kaufman, Texas, the largest training and breeding facility of Tennessee Walking Horses in the Southwest. There he became head trainer and was introduce to many top trainers and owners in the business.

In 2003, he left to open his own training barn and breeding program, Five Star Farms in Royce City, Texas. Smiley's professional degree in psychology gives him unique insight into the psyche of the horse. His training methods, based on communication with the rider and working with each horse as an individual, allows Smiley the amazing ability to nurture each horses God-given potential whether the horse is on the trail or on the rail.

Although they have yet to win a world title, they have had one top three finish and several top ten finishes. It shouldn't be long before Smiley and Five Star Farms rides under the spotlight and hears their name called as Grand Champion of the world.

In addition to training, Five Star Farms has three colorful and talented stallions available for breeding and offers quality Tennessee Walking Horses and Spotted Saddle Horses for sale. Smiley also performs exhibitions at Cowboys of Color Rodeos and speaks to youth and adult organizations about excellence, integrity and pursuing your dreams with determination and joy.

Conclusion

As we mentioned in the acknowledgement, there is no way we could cover all of the wonderful stories that need to be told. This book is just the first in a series of books that will highlight diverse cultures and the contributions they made to the settling of the American West.

The sad reality is that most people today get their history from television and movies...fiction not fact. And for many years, the history books, documented accounts and film versions were mostly one-sided. The stories portrayed were mainly about whites or Europeans, rarely did the stories describe the contributions of Native, Hispanic, Asian or African Americans in any comprehensive or positive light.

The American West was a unique and diversified group of peoples and cultures trying to coexist while carving out their own small or vast piece of this new territory. They lived on their own terms, creating lives out of nothing and leaving a proud legacy for following generations.

Future publications and products will address Indians, Hispanics, Asians and Europeans as well as additional African Americans and their stories. We hope you have enjoyed these profiles and that you will tell your friends and family about them.

If you have someone whose story you think should be told, or questions about these or other contributions to our collective Western heritage, please email us at *Info@WildWestDiversity.com*. You may also follow us on our blog, social networks or sign up for our monthly membership newsletter at *www.LizLawlessCreations.com*. And don't forget...look for us on the trail!

Autographs

Autographs